THE RUSSIAN REVOLUTION

Stewart Ross

Titles in this series

China since 1945
The Cold War
The Origins of the First World War
The Russian Revolution
South Africa since 1948
The Third Reich

Cover illustration: A poster celebrating the second anniversary of the Great October Revolution of 1917.

First published in 1988 by
Wayland (Publishers) Ltd
61 Western Road, Hove
East Sussex BN3 1JD, England

© Copyright 1988 Wayland (Publishers) Ltd

Editor: Kerstin Walker
Designer: Robert Wheeler Associates
Consultant: Beryl Williams, Reader in Russian history at the University of Sussex.

British Library Cataloguing in Publication Data
Ross, Stewart.
    The Russian revolution
    (Witness history).
    1. Soviet union. Political events, 1900–
    1927
    I. Title   II. Series
    947.08′3

    ISBN 1–85210–322–1

Typeset by Kalligraphics Limited, Redhill, Surrey
Printed and bound by Sagdos S.p.A., Milan

Contents

The Russian Empire in 1914

THE RUSSIAN EMPIRE covered about 22 million square kilometres. The area to the west of the Ural mountains, known as European Russia, was bigger than the whole of the rest of Europe, while to the east stretched an area twice as large again. Within the Empire almost every type of climate and geographical feature could be found, from Arctic wastes in the north to the mighty Himalayas in the south, and from arid desert in the east to the rich farmlands of the Ukraine north of the Black Sea. The map below shows how many countries had borders with Russia. It is not difficult to imagine why, in the early part of this century, Russian attitudes towards world problems were studied just as much as they are today.

Because it had been acquired through conquest, the Russian Empire comprised many different races. Only roughly half the population of about 170 million was Russian. Among the remainder were Poles, Georgians, Ukrainians, Cossacks, Jews, White Russians and people of Turkish origin. The Tsarist government followed a policy of Russification, encouraging the nationalities of the Empire to give up their native languages and religions (these included Roman Catholics, Muslims and Buddhists) and adopt the Russian language and the Russian Orthodox faith. This policy caused deep resentment among the minority peoples.

Only about 25 million of the Empire's subjects lived in towns. The urban population was centred around two cities; the ancient capital, Moscow, and St Petersburg

A map of the Russian Empire in the early twentieth century, showing the main railways, major towns and countries bordering it.

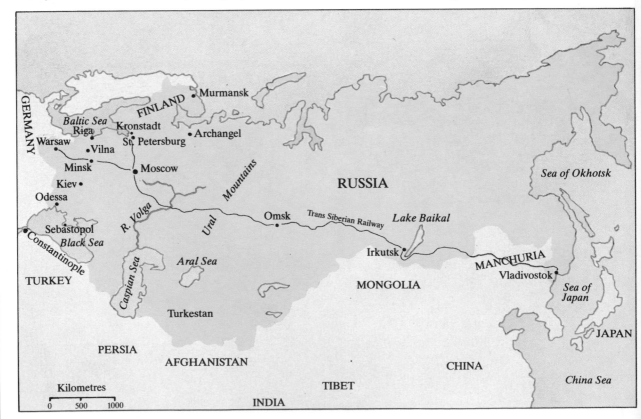

Russian peasants at a village meeting. When serfdom was abolished in 1861 the government gave considerable power to village leaders.

(renamed Petrograd in 1914). There were other centres of population in the industrial areas of the south, in Poland, and in the mining districts in the Urals. St Petersburg had a population approaching 2½ million, and there were about a dozen cities with populations of over 200,000. However, most Russians lived in small villages, either as landless labourers or farming their own small plots. They were at best badly educated, desperately poor and prone to all the diseases that poverty brings. Communica-tions were haphazard, with few adequate roads and a rudimentary railway system. Most Russians knew little of their district, still less of their province, and the concept of the Empire was something that was beyond the comprehension of nearly everyone.

Tsarist rule

During the thirteenth century the Mongols, a fierce nomadic people from Central Asia, had conquered an empire stretching from China to Hungary. Slowly, however, their power declined and new states emerged: the principality of Moscow gained its independence from the Mongols in 1480. Under a number of vigorous leaders, notably Ivan III (1462–1505) and Ivan IV (1533–84), known as 'The Terrible', the huge unified Russian state was carved out. Peter the Great (1682–1725) and Catherine the Great (1762–96), by absorbing Poland and lands bordering the Baltic, made the Russian Empire a Western power. The hereditary leaders of Russia were known as Tsars (or Czars, from the Roman Julius Caesar). They were autocrats, that is to say they were absolute rulers able to do almost as they wished in matters of government.

To assist them in their government, the Tsars employed three major institutions: the Church, the bureaucracy and the police. The Christian Church in Russia had been brought under the control of the state by Peter the Great and, despite attempts at reform in the early twentieth century, the Russian Orthodox Church (the name by which the Church in Russia is known) remained largely an arm of the state. In areas remote from St Petersburg and Moscow it played a major part in the policy of Russification, by persecuting Roman Catholics, Muslims and other religious groups, through its hold over education and through its active encouragement of Russian culture.

The Russian bureaucracy was as inefficient as it was large. Ruling over each of the Empire's provinces was a Provincial Governor and below him ran a bewilderingly complex chain of command, often overlapping, down to humble village officials. The whole ramshackle organization was obsessed with paperwork, uniforms, rank and formality. Concern for the good government of the state was often the lowest priority.

Tsar Nicholas II (centre) and his wife Alexandra at the celebrations in 1913 to mark the three-hundred-year anniversary of their ruling dynasty, the Romanovs. Alexis, their son and heir, is being held by a Cossack bodyguard. The young boy suffered from haemophilia.

Finally, a large police force, the Okhrana, which operated both secretly and openly, existed to enforce law and order and protect the government.

Yet in the fifty or so years before the outbreak of the First World War, the Russian Empire had been changing fast. In the 1860s serfdom had been abolished and representative institutions for local government had been set up. The economy boomed. Finally, following a revolution in 1905, Tsar Nicholas II had permitted the establishment of a national representative institution called the Duma – a sort of parliament with very limited powers and a limited franchise. With this came political parties, elections, a freer press and a massive campaign to educate the Russian people. But the Tsar was an unwilling reformer who had had change thrust upon him. In August 1914 his Empire still faced as much back to the nineteenth century as it did forward into the future.

► A poster produced by Victor Deni in 1919. It is a caricature of the Russian Orthodox Church entitled 'Fly Catcher and Booty'. Who is the fly catcher and who is the booty? What does it suggest about the artist's attitude towards the Church?

▼ Troops firing on the crowds in St Petersburg during the 1905 revolution. Later in the year the loyalty even of the troops was doubtful, and the Tsar was forced to yield to the moderate demands of some revolutionaries.

The Russian economy

In 1914 Russian agriculture was changing quite rapidly. Until 1861 the great majority of peasants who lived on the land were serfs: they were landless labourers, owned either by the state or by a wealthy individual. After emancipation most peasants remained desperately poor, and industrial expansion was given a higher priority by the government than agricultural development. For example, corn was exported to earn much needed foreign currency, even though there was a shortage of it at home. Peasant unrest was to play a major part in the 1905 revolution.

After 1906 Peter Stolypin, the new Minister of the Interior, introduced a series of measures that attempted to solve the 'peasant problem'. By 1914 they were beginning to have some effect. Stolypin's laws encouraged private ownership of land and the consolidation of individual holdings into single farms. Harvests were good, production rose and more land was brought under cultivation. The use of fertilizers and machinery increased. By 1916 perhaps half the peasant households owned their own land.

By 1914 Russian industry was expanding even faster than her agriculture. The value

A Russian textile factory in the Kineshma province on the Volga in 1910. Although this machinery was the very latest in technology, the Russians were extremely short of skilled operators and maintenance engineers.

of imports and exports rose by 50 per cent between 1909 and 1913, and during the same period coal output increased from 25.5 to 35.5 million tonnes. The latest machinery was imported from the west and many of Russia's factories, such as that shown opposite, were very efficient. There is some evidence, too, that the economy was becoming less dependent than it had been upon a few key industries, such as railways, as the Russians started to produce electrical and other manufactured goods.

However, historians have been arguing for over fifty years as to the true nature of Russia's economic progress. Much of her industry was owned by foreigners; half the coal industry, for example, was in French hands. Secondly, although Russia was

Russian agriculture struggled towards modernization in the early twentieth century, but despite improvements in farming techniques the traditional plough was still widely used in 1914.

developing fast, she was being outstripped by the other major industrial nations. Finally, Russian labour was largely unskilled and still desperately poor. Industrial workers regarded their roots as still being in their villages, while on the land there was resentment against the few who had done well out of Stolypin's changes. The annual death rate in Russia was twice that of England, the average income six times less than that in the USA. On the eve of the First World War the outlook for the Russian economy was at best uncertain.

1914

If Russia was to cope with the various problems that confronted her in 1914, she needed two things: able leadership and peace. But she had neither of these. The 46-year-old Tsar, although a devoted husband and a loving father, had neither the skill nor the understanding to guide his country through the transition to a modern state. His strong sense of duty all too often seemed mere obstinacy. His wife, Alexandra, was a much more forceful personality, but she was devoted to upholding autocracy and thus reinforced her husband's conservatism. Moreover, as a German, she was unpopular and her influence over her husband was resented.

Opposition to Nicholas's government was widespread, but few of the hostile groups shared the same aims. The most moderate opposition came from the Constitutional Democrats, (the Cadets), led by Pavel Miliukov. This group was prominent in the Duma, calling for western-style liberal reforms, such as equal suffrage. Some Cadets were republicans.

Operating outside the Duma, and usually outside the law, were more extreme groups. The most radical were the anarchists, or nihilists, who rejected all government as immoral and corrupt. The largest and most popular revolutionary party was the Socialist Revolutionary Party, (the S.R.s), whose followers held a wide range of ideas, some socialist ones from the west, others inherited from the older populist movement. This held that the future for Russia lay with its own culture and virtues, which were to be found in the peasantry. The S.R.s called for revolution, both among the peasants and the new urban working classes. To help bring this about they followed a policy of terror through their 'battle section'. In 1911 this group, after four years of lying low, assassinated Stolypin, heralding a new phase of violence and strikes that was to last until the outbreak of war in 1914.

The Social Democrats were a second

Vladimir Ilyich Lenin (1870–1924), the leader of the Bolshevik party, who played a part in the 1905 revolution before fleeing abroad. This prolific revolutionary writer and organizer remained in Switzerland until 1917.

revolutionary party. They were split between the more moderate Mensheviks (in the minority), led by Julius Martov, and the Bolsheviks (in the majority). This group, whose leader was Vladimir Lenin, believed that a successful revolution in Russia could be organized only by a small dedicated band of professional Marxist revolutionaries. Until 1917 such an idea seemed far-fetched.

In the first half of 1914, 1,250,000 workers came out on strike as revolutionary activity escalated. Then, on 1 August Germany declared war on Russia. This came about because Russia stood by her Balkan ally, Serbia, against the threats of Austria-Hungary and Germany. As war seemed inevitable, Germany decided to strike first. Faced with a common enemy, the Russian people temporarily shelved their differences. Only the exiled Lenin wryly commented that a war was 'a very useful thing for revolution'.

This photograph shows Russian women hauling timber rafts on a river. How do you think such people would react to the calls of the revolutionaries, offering them personal dignity and their own land to farm?

The fall of the Romanovs 1914–17

SINCE 1894 RUSSIA had been allied to France. When war broke out in 1914 the Russian Generals Samsonov and Rennenkampf attacked Germany through East Prussia to take pressure off their hard-pressed ally, France, in the west. They were disastrously defeated at the battles of Tannenburg and the Masurian Lakes in 1914. Further south a successful attack against Austria was counter-balanced by a German offensive into Poland. When Turkey joined the Central Powers in the autumn of 1914, Russia found herself at war on two fronts.

By the end of 1915, a massive German and Austrian offensive had pushed General Alekseev's army out of Poland and back to a line east of Riga and Vilna. Meanwhile, the inexperienced Nicholas II had taken personal command of his armies, replacing the incompetent General Sukhomlinov. An allied landing at Gallipoli, to relieve the eastern allies, was a complete failure. To make matters worse, in October 1915 Bulgaria joined the Central Powers, and Serbia, in whose defence Russia had originally gone to war, was crushed. The next year the Germans were tied up in the west, and Russian offensives by General Brusilov into Galicia (in Austria) made considerable headway. Although by the beginning of 1917 the Russian military situation was not disastrous, the cost of the fighting, in terms of men, equipment and goodwill towards the government, had been enormous.

When war broke out a powerful wave of patriotism had swept across Russia, ending strikes and uniting all classes in the war effort. But defeat and ineffective organization soon fuelled opposition to the war. For a time, in 1915, 25 per cent of Russian soldiers were sent to battle unarmed, told to collect what they could in the way of weapons from the dead. Ministers came and went in rapid succession; in twelve months of 1915–16 there were five Ministers of the Interior. A ban on liquor sales, which was supposed to help efficiency, served only to deprive the government of their largest source of revenue. Inflation rose and there were severe shortages of fuel and food, particularly in the cities. Criticism of the government mounted. In 1916 a huge armed rebellion broke out in Central Asia; in December Rasputin, the Tsarina's favour-

◄ In the spring and summer of 1915 the Russian army suffered huge losses. The army was poorly trained and equipped and demoralization became worse with every new setback. No one knows exactly how many Russians died in the First World War: the figure is probably around 1,650,000.

► Russian prisoners of war boarding a train near Lvov in June 1915. What do you imagine would be the effect on morale in the Russian army of such scenes of defeat and humiliation?

ite, was assassinated by an aristocratic faction. By the end of the year there was once again talk of revolution.

The first revolution of 1917 started with riots in Petrograd on 8 March. The rioters soon joined with strikers from a local factory, and troops who were ordered to put down the unrest refused to do so. Nicholas was away at the front and unable to do anything. Within a few days government of the country had come to a halt as protestors broke into jails, police stations and public buildings. Ignoring an order to dissolve, the Duma set up its own Provisional Government under Prince Lvov on 12 March. Cadets, socialists and conservatives all joined it. Realizing that he no longer commanded the loyalty of his soldiers and civil servants, Nicholas II abdicated for himself and his son on 15 March. His brother, Grand Duke Michael, refused to accept the throne, and so ended the Russian monarchy.

How secure was the regime in 1914?

When we look at Russia in 1914 we know that the government of the Romanovs collapsed in 1917, so we are tempted to say that the Tsar's regime was bound to fail. This was not necessarily so.

During the celebrations to mark the three hundredth anniversary of the Romanov dynasty, the Tsar and his wife travelled along the Volga River to the place where his ancestor had been elected to the throne in March 1613. The Grand Duchess Olga Alexandrovna recalled the trip:

> *Wherever we went we met with manifestations of loyalty bordering on wildness. When our steamer went down the Volga we saw crowds of peasants wading waist high in the water to catch a glimpse of Nicky. In some of the towns I would see artisans and workmen falling down to kiss his shadow as we passed. Cheers were deafening.*[1]

What does this comment from a Grand Duchess suggest to us about the Tsar's popularity? Would a Grand Duchess be a reliable source of information on the feelings of the ordinary Russians? Perhaps people in the industrial slums of St Petersburg or Moscow thought differently from the peasants along the Volga.

How do the thoughts of the Grand Duchess compare with the statement of the historian George Florovsky?

> *. . . actually the main weakness of the Russian monarchy of the imperial period consisted not at all in representing the interests of a 'minority' . . . but in the fact that it represented no one whatsoever.*[2]

Even Lenin at the beginning of 1917 had not expected revolution to come so soon. In January 1917 he said, 'We, the old, will probably not live to see the decisive battles of the coming revolution.'[3]

We have seen on page 6 how by 1914 Russian industry was expanding and how some sections of the peasantry were beginning to assemble profitable, efficient farms. We have also noted how the government was placing much emphasis on education, seeking to have a wholly literate population by 1922.

Now examine the photograph below, taken of a dormitory for women workers in a textile mill in Moscow. These were the

A women's hostel of the Prokhorov textile mills in Moscow. How would you describe life in these conditions?

living conditions of some of the workers who were producing Russia's industrial revolution. They often still considered themselves village folk, who came into the towns to find work.

Imagine a worker living in such a dormitory, who had been taught to read, seeing this cartoon above, produced by the Social Democrats in 1900. One does not have to be able to read Russian to guess at the meaning of the labels of the different levels of

A cartoon produced by the Social Democrats. Can you identify each layer of Russian society depicted in the picture?

society. Who are the class at the bottom, holding up the rest of society? Does the situation seem fair? It is often said that revolutions do not occur when people are at their lowest ebb, but when things are improving and there is hope of still better to come if only changes can be made.

15

Nicholas and Alexandra

The Tsar of Russia appointed and dismissed his ministers and had the final word in important decisions in both domestic and foreign policy. He did not have to listen to the Duma's advice and he could govern perfectly well without it.

This picture captures two sides of Nicholas II's personality; his strong sense of duty and his love for his family. The photograph shows him about to set out with Alexis on a long march to test the Russian soldier's uniform and equipment.

Such enormous power in the hands of a single person worked well if the Tsar was exceptionally able. For example, Peter the Great (Tsar 1682–1725), an energetic ruler, used his authority to make Russia a western power. But even Peter would have found the military, industrial, political and social problems confronting Russia in 1914 difficult to deal with. Therefore, at this crucial point in her history Russia needed an exceptional leader. Was Nicholas II such a person?

When he heard of the sudden death of his father Tsar Nicholas burst out:

> What am I going to do? What is going to happen to me? . . . I am not prepared to be a Tsar. I never wanted to become one. I know nothing of the business of ruling.[6]

Yet, within a few days the 26-year-old Tsar was stating his principles clearly:

> Let all know that I, devoting all my strength to the welfare of the people, will uphold the principle of autocracy as firmly and as unflinchingly as my late unforgettable father.[7]

It is important to consider whether such a tough attitude, from a man who had been so uncertain about his job, was the wisest position to adopt at a time of change.

The Tsarina Alexandra had a powerful personality. She encouraged her husband in his beliefs. 'Forgive me, precious one,' she wrote to him in April 1915, 'but you know you are too kind and gentle . . . do, my love, be more decided and sure of yourself.'[8]

Nicholas and Alexandra's son, Alexis, heir to the Russian throne, suffered from haemophilia. In those days there was little that medical science could do to help the

16

boy. However, it was discovered that Rasputin, a peasant monk, had strange powers that could bring the Tsarevitch relief from pain, and because of this the healer became a court favourite, especially with Alexandra.

A number of scandalous stories were spread about this uncouth monk and his friendship with the Tsarina. All of Russia knew how Rasputin took advantage of his position at court, and about his womanizing and his drunkenness, but Alexandra would not listen to these stories. She was obsessed only with the man's ability to help her son. In the end a group of patriotic young aristocrats murdered Rasputin in December 1916. But by then the reputation of the royal family had been seriously damaged.

► The Tsar and the Tsarevitch in their uniforms. What sort of image do you think they are trying to create?

▼ Rasputin (seated) surrounded by some of his female admirers. It was resentment of his influence at court and stories of his womanizing that eventually led to Rasputin's downfall.

Defeat

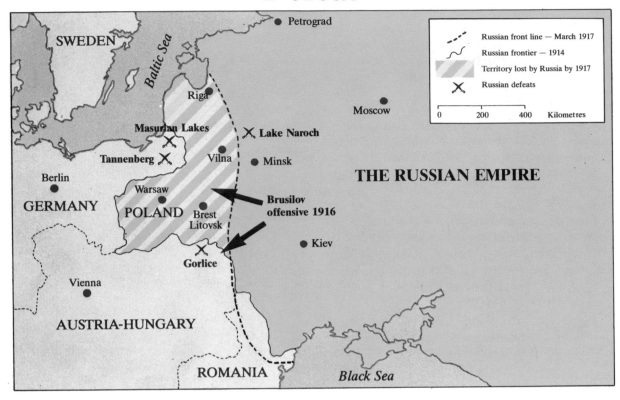

A map showing Russian territorial losses between 1914 and 1917.

The unstable situation in Russia in 1914 was made much worse by the war. The first point about Russia's role in the war is that most of her allies expected her to do well. The large Russian armies were nicknamed 'the steamroller', slow to get going but unstoppable once in operation. In fact the Russian armies mobilized much quicker than military observers had anticipated, and, following a series of reforms after 1905, they were in reasonably good shape. But would they prove unstoppable?

The map above shows just what did happen to the Russian armies between 1914 and 1917. Clearly a good deal of territory was lost. But defeat can have one of two effects on a country, just as it can on a football team. Either it can inspire people to greater efforts, or it can cause them to lose heart and give up. When does defeat inspire greater efforts?

A When the scale of the defeat is not too great;

B When the leaders have the confidence of their followers;

C When there is great loyalty to the cause.

Let us look at these three factors in the case of Russia:

A The scale of the loss. The amount of territory lost is shown by the map above. Human casualties are illustrated in the following table:

Total number in Russian army	15,000,000
Killed in battle	1,300,000
Wounded	4,200,000
Died of wounds	350,000
Taken prisoner	2,417,000

What percentage of the total number of soldiers called upon to fight were either killed, wounded or captured? Can any army suffering such large losses continue fighting?

B Leadership. In the light of the figures above, consider this letter written in 1916 from the Tsarina Alexandra to her husband, the Tsar, in which she encourages him to greater effort:

> *Be firm . . . one wants to feel your hand – how long, years, people have told me the same 'Russia loves to feel the whip' – it's their nature – tender love and then the iron hand to punish and guide.*[4]

The Tsar loved his wife dearly and often listened to her advice. Do you think letters like this were a wise response to the military situation in 1916?

C Loyalty. The photograph below, taken in 1917, shows a Russian soldier using his rifle to arrest two deserters. What does it suggest about the state of discipline and morale in the Russian army?

It can be concluded that the war did play an important part in the collapse of the Tsarist regime in 1917. But remember, Russia was not knocked out of the war in March 1917. Her armies were intact and in the previous year they had had some success, although it was probably unwise for them to have tried to advance. The Russians had always done best when defending their homeland, aided by their severe winters and the huge distances their enemies had to cover. In fact, the revolution was not

Examine this poster produced in 1918. The Tsar, the Church and the rich are being carried away by the Russian people. What is the artist trying to suggest about the Tsar's leadership and the state of the Russian people at this time? How would the artist react to the statement by the Tsarina Alexandra that 'Russia loves to feel the whip'?

started by soldiers. There were other factors at work, perhaps equally as important as the defeat of the Russian armies, in undermining the Tsar's government.

A loyal Russian soldier using his rifle to arrest two deserters.

19

The strains of war

Nicholas II was forced to abdicate by the refusal of the Russian people from all walks of life, particularly those living in Petrograd, to co-operate any longer with his government. We have seen how incompetent command and poor supply led to the Russian armies being forced to retreat deep into Russia, having suffered terrible casualties. The reaction of the Russian people to this was not so much despair, as anger.

Consider the picture opposite. It captures the feelings of soldiers returning home maimed and wounded from the front, to find chaos and desolation at home. Whom would the troops be likely to blame? The soldiers' anger was matched by that of the city dwellers, who were also having to endure severe hardships in order to support the general war effort.

In July 1915 Tsar Nicholas wrote to his wife, Alexandra:

> *Again that cursed question of shortage of artillery and rifle ammunition – it stands in the way of an energetic advance. If we should have three days of serious fighting we might run out of ammunition altogether.*[5]

▲ A soldier returning home from the front at the end of the First World War to find his house and village destroyed.

▼ By March 1917 disillusionment with the Tsar's government and the war effort was high. This was the first demonstration in Petrograd, in front of the monument to Alexander III. Already flags bearing the portraits and slogans of the revolution can be seen.

Citizens of Petrograd queueing outside a bakery in 1917, waiting to buy bread.

To pay for more ammunition and weapons, the government printed more banknotes. This led to a rapid rise in prices (food prices, for example, rose 300 per cent). But the peasants, who produced the grain that fed the cities such as Petrograd, were not paid any more for their produce, so they hoarded it, waiting for better times. The result of this is clear in the photograph above. The queue is waiting outside a bakery in Petrograd.

Bread was not the only commodity in short supply. As factories were turned over to the manufacture of military supplies, there were shortages of all basic items, from clothes to fuel. To make matters worse, even when food and goods were available there was rarely sufficient transport to take them to the cities. The priority of the railways, for example, was supplying the front.

Wages had risen by 100 per cent, much less than prices, so what goods were available cost much more than they had done before the war. Discontent mounted. The Germans were not slow to take advantage of the situation, supplying money to revolutionaries who stirred the Russian workers to strike.

In a democratic country, when the people are disatisfied with the government they can show their feelings in an election, which gives them the opportunity to change the government. The Russians had no such power. They had to express their wishes in other ways.

Therefore, by February 1917 the situation was as follows:

- The Russian army had done less well than people expected and had suffered very heavy losses.
- The strain of supplying the army had disrupted the Russian economy, causing major shortages and hardship, particularly in the cities. The Germans encouraged this discontent.
- With mounting fury, the Russian people asked who was responsible for their humiliation and misery.

March–November 1917

THE PROVISIONAL GOVERNMENT formed itself on 12 March 1917. Although its nominal leader was the aristocrat Prince George Lvov, the majority of its leaders came from the Duma. P. N. Miliukov, an historian and leader of the Constitutional Democrats, became Minister of Foreign Affairs. The conservative A. I. Guchkov was given the post of Minister of War and of the Navy, while Alexander Kerensky, the only Socialist Party member in the cabinet, became Minister of Justice. However, the leaders of the government held differing views, and at the same time as they had established themselves workers and revolutionaries in towns all over Russia had set up elected assemblies, called Soviets. These committees issued their own orders independently of the Provisional Government.

Although well-intentioned, the Provisional Government misjudged the mood of the Russian people. It did little to deal with the hardships of war and starvation that beset the major cities; street demonstrations against government policy, such as that shown here in Petrograd, were common.

The Provisional Government promised much but achieved little. It was not democratically elected and failed to hold elections for a representative assembly. The peasants were not satisfied with mere promises of more land. Meanwhile, the war dragged on. Urged on by Kerensky, in late June General Brusilov began another offensive in the south-west. The troops were unwilling to fight and thousands mutinied as the Russians were driven back by both the German and Austrian armies. In May Miliukov and

Guchkov left the cabinet, to be followed by more moderate members in July. Before the end of the month Lvov himself had resigned and Kerensky was left to lead a largely socialist ministry.

The Provisional Government hoped to establish a western-style democracy in Russia. Most censorship was abolished, local government was made more democratic, political prisoners were set free, and national minorities were given greater self-government. However, using their new-found freedom to express themselves, groups of soldiers and sailors in Petrograd, supported by mobs of citizens, joined an attempt by the Bolsheviks to seize power between 16 and 18 July. The 'July days', considered by Lenin to be ill-timed, were a failure and many Bolshevik leaders fled or were arrested.

Following the failure of a State Conference of representatives from many different Russian organizations, ranging from local governments to the Soviets, the country's crisis deepened. In September General Kornilov attempted a right wing *coup d'état*, but was thwarted when Kerensky appealed to the people to 'save the revolution'. The Bolshevik Red Guard played an important part in blocking General Kornilov's advance on Petrograd. The Bolsheviks now attracted greater popular support; by the end of September they were in a majority on both the Petrograd and Moscow Soviets. Lenin sensed the time was right. On the night of 6–7 November the Bolsheviks seized key points in Petrograd, and the second revolution of 1917 had begun.

Ten of the original members of the Provisional Government. Prince Lvov is top row, centre, Kerensky is top row, second from right, Guchkov bottom row, centre, and Miliukov bottom row, second left. The coalition of ministers holding widely differing political views was not a success and few of the original twelve were left in office by November 1917.

People and policies

The Provisional Government was replaced by a Communist dictatorship after only eight months in power. The reasons why this happened can be examined under two headings: the failures of the Provisional Government, and the strength of their Bolshevik successors. In this section we will look at the former, leaving the Bolsheviks to the next section.

The socialist Kerensky, the most able politician to serve in the Provisional Government, claimed in his *Memoirs* that:

> *During the very first days of its existence, the Provisional Government began to receive from every corner of Russia, from large towns and remote villages, as well as from the front, a stream of jubilant messages of support.*[9]

Most of the government's eleven members had emerged from the Duma, to which they had been elected by no more than a tiny fraction of the Russian population. If they did receive the support that Kerensky claims, is it not likely that it was more a measure of relief that the Tsar's rule was over, than approval for the new ministry? Nicholas II's government had been associated with defeat, starvation, inequality and repression. The Provisional Government, many believed, would change all this. Much was expected of it.

Almost as soon as it met, the Provisional Government promised to allow free elections for a representative assembly. But it could not organize elections with millions of men fighting at the front. The government also said that the assembly would offer a fair deal to the peasants in the way land was distributed. But how could it begin to

A May Day demonstration in Petrograd in 1917, protesting against the Provisional Government. What is the significance of soldiers and workers marching together?

redistribute land with millions of farmers in the army? What would have been the effect on the army if the government had released plans to transfer land?

To make matters, worse, as one historian has written:

> *The economic problems with which Russia was faced by 1917, after nearly three years of war, were inherited by the Provisional Government. This proved beyond its capacity to resolve . . . At the end of June a special conference on supply for defence purposes, set up by the government, concluded that 'the state of industry is catastrophic'.*[10]

One of the first acts of the Provisional Government had been to make strikes legal. A number of demonstrations took place in the summer of 1917, in which opponents of

A demonstration in Petrograd in favour of continuing the war effort. Blind war victims are being guided by a nurse as they parade a banner saying 'War until total victory. Long live freedom!' Why did they want to continue the war?

the Provisional Government protested at the new ministry's lack of achievement. Most, such as the one shown opposite, attracted great enthusiasm and participation. There were some patriotic counter-demonstrations, supporting the Provisional Government and the continuation of the war effort, such as the one above. Compare the two demonstrations shown. Russians had expected great changes from the Provisional Government, but what had they achieved by July 1917?

War continued

A women's battalion was used for propaganda purposes to boost morale in the Russian army. Although sent to the front line they did not fight.

They can be seen here being blessed by the head of the Russian Orthodox Church in July 1917, before being sent to the front.

The first and most important aim of the Provisional Government, wrote Kerensky in his *Memoirs*, was 'to continue the defence of the country'.[11] In other words, the Provisional Government promised to continue the war.

Lvov, Kerensky and other members of the cabinet wished to establish a Russian democracy. Therefore, they needed the support of their western democratic allies and they felt they had a duty to continue the struggle against Germany.

But the cost of the war was high. At the front, in particular, matters were deteriorating fast:

Supplies to the army were alarmingly short, as figures based on official reports eloquently testify. Shells, clothing, horseshoes, indeed all necessities, fell below requirements by fifty or sixty per cent, and in some cases even more . . . By October many parts of the army literally faced starvation.[12]

Was the Provisional Government wise to fight on under these conditions?

On 14 March, 1917 the Petrograd Soviet issued its first order. The fourth paragraph read:

The orders of the military commission of the State Duma shall be executed only in such cases as they do not conflict with the orders and resolutions of the Soviet of Workers' and Soldiers' Deputies.

The order told all members of the armed forces to obey the Provisional Government's orders only if the Soviet confirmed them!

What is more, the Bolsheviks on the Soviet were demanding peace. Unwilling to miss a good opportunity, the Germans sent the Bolsheviks money. They also permitted the Bolshevik leader, Lenin, to return from Switzerland to Russia, via Sweden, across Germany in a sealed train. Morale, as Kerensky said, was low:

Everything that was happening in the army at the moment – insubordination, the mutinies, the conversion to Bolshevism of whole units, the endless political meetings, and the mass desertion – was the natural outcome of the terrible conflict in the mind of each soldier . . . The men . . . were overcome by an almost unconquerable urge to drop their weapons and flee from the trenches.[13]

Some soldiers deserted the army. Others, as the picture above shows, turned with friendly greetings towards their enemy.

Perhaps the Provisional Government had made a terrible misjudgement in continuing the war. But what else could it have done?

▲ Russian soldiers sharing their soup with men from the Austrian army in 1917.

▼ A car seized by revolutionaries on patrol in Petrograd who are seeking to drive out any counter-revolutionary forces.

Growing isolation

For the eight months that the Provisional Government was in power parties of all shades of opinion claimed that they had the answer to Russia's problems. Some of the most important were:

- Monarchists, who wished to see a return to rule by the Tsar.
- Octobrists, who were a conservative party formed during the 1905 revolution. In 1915 they joined the 'Progressive Bloc' of parties in the Duma. Guchkov led them in the Provisional Government.
- Cadets, whose name was a shortened form of Constitutional Democrats. This party of middle-class liberals wished to see an English-style constitutional government in Russia. Miliukov was their leader, and they formed the majority of the first Provisional Government.
- Socialists, led by Kerensky. This group,

sometimes known as the Labour Party, was not widely popular in Russia but it was increasingly well represented in the Provisional Government. They had by now joined the Social Revolutionaries.

- Social Democrats, a group of Marxists who had split in 1903 into the Bolsheviks and Mensheviks. In fact the Mensheviks, who believed in gradual progress to a socialist state, had a greater following than the Bolsheviks until 1918. The Menshevik Tseretelli served in the Provisional Government. The Bolsheviks were increasingly popular among factory workers. By the autumn of 1917 their

The first All-Russian Congress of Soviets (shown below) met in Petrograd in June 1917. The presence of such popular alternative sources of authority made the task of the Provisional Government increasingly difficult.

ИЗВѢСТІЯ
ПЕТРОГРАДСКАГО СОВѢТА
Рабочихъ депутатовъ.

№ 1.—28 Февраля 1917 года.   № 1.

Къ населенію Петрограда и Россіи.
Отъ Совѣта Рабочихъ Депутатовъ.

Старая власть довела страну до полнаго развала, а народъ до голоданія. Терпѣть дальше стало невозможно. Населеніе Петрограда вышло на улицу, чтобы заявить о своемъ недовольствѣ. Его встрѣтили залпами. Вмѣсто хлѣба царское правительство дало народу свинецъ.

Но солдаты не захотѣли итти противъ народа и возстали противъ правительства. Вмѣстѣ съ народомъ они захватили оружіе, военные склады и рядъ важныхъ правительственныхъ учрежденій.

Борьба еще продолжается; она должна быть доведена до конца. Старая власть должна быть окончательно низвергнута и уступить мѣсто народному правленію. Въ этомъ спасеніе Россіи.

Для успѣшнаго завершенія борьбы въ интересахъ демократіи народъ долженъ создать свою собственную властную организацію.

Вчера 27 февраля въ столицѣ образовался Совѣтъ Рабочихъ Депутатовъ—изъ выборныхъ представителей заводовъ и фабрикъ, возставшихъ воинскихъ частей, а также демократическихъ и соціалистическихъ партій и группъ.

Совѣтъ Рабочихъ Депутатовъ засѣдающій въ Государственной Думѣ ставитъ своей основной задачей организацію народныхъ силъ и борьбу за окончательное упроченіе политической свободы и народнаго правленія въ Россіи.

Совѣтъ назначилъ районныхъ комиссаровъ для установленія народной власти въ районахъ Петрограда.

Приглашаемъ все населеніе столицы немедленно сплотиться вокругъ Совѣта, образовать мѣстные комитеты въ районахъ и взять въ свои руки управленіе всѣми мѣстными дѣлами.

Всѣ вмѣстѣ, общими силами будемъ бороться за полное устраненіе стараго правительства и созывъ учредительнаго собранія, избраннаго на основѣ всеобщаго равнаго, прямого и тайнаго избирательнаго права.

Совѣтъ Рабочихъ Депутатовъ.

6

NEWS OF THE
PETROGRAD SOVIET
of Workmen Deputies.

№ 1 — March 13, 1917   № 1

To the population of Petrograd and Russia
From the Soviet of Workmen's Deputies.

The old authorities brought the country to ruin and the people to starvation. It became impossible to endure it longer. The population of Petrograd came out in the streets to express its discontent. It was met with guns. Instead of bread, the government of the Czar gave the people bullets.

But the soldiers have refused to go against the people and have revolted against the government. Together with the civilians they have seized the armories the military stores and many important government institutions.

The struggle is still going on; it must be brought to an end. The old power must be deposed and replaced by a people's government. This is the salvation of Russia.

To secure a victorious end of this struggle in the interests of democracy, the people must create an organization of its own power.

Yesterday, March the 12th, a Soviet of Workmen Deputies was formed in the Capital. It consists of representatives elected from the shops and factories, the revolting military detachments and also from democratic and socialist parties and groups.

The Soviet of Workmen Deputies now in session at the Imperial Duma faces as its basic problem, the organization of the people's forces in the battle for permanent political freedom and self-government in Russia.

The Soviet has appointed district commissars to execute the people's authority in the districts of Petrograd.

We call upon the inhabitants of the capital to rally around the Soviet, to form district committees and to take the administration of local affairs in their own hands.

All together, we unite our forces to fight for the complete destruction of the old government, and for the calling of a Constituent Assembly, elected on the basis of a universal, equal, direct and secret ballot.

The Soviet of Workers' Deputies.

[*This is a reproduction in English of the Russian text on the opposite page.*]

belief that a second, communist revolution had to be organized for Russia by a small band of revolutionaries was no longer looking as far-fetched as it had done.

- Social Revolutionaries (S.R.s), who were popular among the peasants, demanded, among other things, the abolition of the private ownership of land. Victor Chernov, who joined the first Provisional Government, was their most influential leader.

If you find this list confusing, remember that the Russians were also bewildered by all these parties and their conflicting claims. John Reed, an American journalist serving in Petrograd at the time, found the situation 'extremely confusing', especially as most of the groups mentioned above sprouted smaller, breakaway sections.[14]

Now consider the task of the Provisional Government. Its authority was challenged by the Soviet on the grounds that it had not been elected and therefore had no real right to be governing the country, although the

The first issue of a news-sheet by the Petrograd Soviet.

Provisional Government later changed its membership to introduce more socialist representatives.

Examine the news-sheet above, issued by the Petrograd Soviet on 13 March, in which it challenges the authority of the Provisional Government just one day after it had been formed.

1 Why does it challenge the authority of the Provisional Government?
2 What are the demands of the Soviet?
3 What effect would these challenges have on the position and role of the Provisional Government?

The Provisional Government had failed to deal with the problems of war, land and famine. Perhaps Kerensky was trying to change from an autocracy to a democracy too fast. Maybe only a new authoritarian government could cope with the chaotic situation of 1917.

The Bolshevik Revolution

Lenin addressing crowds of soldiers in 1920. The revolution of November 1917 was essentially Lenin's revolution. He alone had the political insight to realize that the time had come for the Bolsheviks to seize power, and his brilliant oratory urged waverers to adopt the Bolshevik cause.

THE REMARKABLE FEATURE about November 1917 is the way in which the Bolshevik leader Lenin moved to the centre of the stage of Russian history, a position he maintained until his death in 1924. Lenin had been in hiding in Finland since July; then, on 23 October, he returned to Petrograd in disguise. He was convinced that the time was right for the Bolsheviks to seize power. After hours of discussion he won over Zinoviev, Kamenev and all but two of the twelve-man Bolshevik Central Committee. Lenin was ably supported by Lev Trotsky, who held the influential position of chairman of the Petrograd Soviet. Preparations now went ahead for the coup. Rifles were handed out to the Bolshevik Red Guard. The Bolshevik crew of the cruiser *Aurora*, stationed on Petrograd's Neva river, made ready, and Trotsky won over the soldiers of the city's Peter and Paul fortress.

Kerensky finally moved against the Bolsheviks on 6 November, but his action was too late. That night Red Guards seized key positions throughout Petrograd. The next day they dissolved Kerensky's half-hearted pre-Parliament and later arrested the members of the Provisional Government who had been sheltering in the feebly defended Winter Palace. Kerensky fled the city. The second All-Russian Congress of Soviets had also met on 7 November. Controlled by the Bolsheviks, who held 390 of its 650 seats, it told Soviets throughout Russia to assume power. In many cities the command was obeyed.

Swiftly and with great authority Lenin now set about establishing his government and introducing the changes he had promised. Government was placed in the hands of the Bolshevik party, led by its twelve-man Politbureau, and a cabinet known as the Council of People's Commissars. It was supported by a ruthless secret police, Cheka. In January the long-awaited Constituent Assembly met, but when Lenin discovered that of the 707 members only 170 were Bolsheviks, he ordered his troops to dissolve it.

The Bolsheviks introduced a number of reforms in rapid succession. Peasant families were given enough land to farm, the Church was stripped of all wealth and power, banks were nationalized, titles and ranks were abolished, women were made fully equal with men. The calendar was brought into line with the rest of Europe, and new courts replaced the existing judicial system. Finally, on 3 March 1918 peace was made with Germany at Brest-Litovsk. Its terms were humiliating, forcing Russia to hand over 60 million people, 27 per cent of her arable land, and 33 per cent of her manufacturing industry. But by the spring of 1918 the Bolsheviks faced enough problems without having to fight a foreign war as well.

▶ Red Guards storming the Winter Palace, where the Provisional Government was based. The palace was easily taken, but the somewhat disorganized soldiers took a little while to find the deposed ministers who were sheltering in a room deep within the building.

▼ Troops loyal to the Provisional Government guarding a Petrograd telephone exchange in October 1917. When the Bolsheviks took over such buildings a month later none of the troops offered armed resistance.

The November Revolution

The Provisional Government is absolutely powerless. The bourgeoisie is in control . . . Now, during the Revolution, one sees revolts of peasants who are tired of waiting for their promised land; and all over the country, in all the toiling classes, the same disgust is evident . . . The Army is with us. The conciliators and pacifists, Socialist Revolutionaries, and Mensheviks, have lost all authority – because the struggle between the peasants and the landlords, between the workers and employers, between the soldiers and officers, has become more bitter . . . only by the victory of the proletarian dictatorship, can the Revolution be achieved and the people saved . . .[15]

This speech was made by Trotsky, the influential Bolshevik leader, on 30 October 1917. Imagine the impact of these words on the average Russian citizen, worker, soldier or peasant. In simple terms, the Bolsheviks spread their brilliant propaganda:

All power to the Soviets both in the capital and in the provinces. Immediate truce on all fronts. An honest peace between peoples. Landlord estates – without compensation – to the peasants. Workers' control over industrial production. A faithfully and honestly elected Constituent Assembly.[16]

A Bolshevik propaganda poster designed to win over Cossacks. On the left is a Red peasant, a soldier and a worker and on the right are the landlords, the generals and the capitalists. What are the two choices laid before the Cossack in this poster? Which do you think would have a more popular appeal and why?

In Lenin's own words, the Bolshevik programme boiled down to two simple slogans: 'All power to the Soviets!' and 'Peace, Bread, Land!' The attraction of the simple Bolshevik slogans for people who had suffered so much was considerable.

John Reed gives these election figures for local government in Moscow, comparing June 1917 with September:

	June	September
S.R.s	58	14
Cadets	17	30
Mensheviks	12	4
Bolsheviks	11	47 [17]

Seeing the way the tide was moving, the Bolsheviks moved into action. The map below shows the stages by which they seized Petrograd. The city was well provided with garrisons of troops. Why did none rally to Kerensky? In discussing why the Bolsheviks succeeded so easily the following points are worth bearing in mind:

1 'There was no cut-and-dried plan of insurrection. Everything points to the fact that seizure of power was improvised around events as they developed.'[18]

2 The seizure of the city on the night of 6–7 November was presented to the Second Congress of Soviets, meeting at 10.40 a.m. in Petrograd on 7 November.

3 As one general reported, 'The government had no troops at its disposal.' Most remained neutral. Bolshevik propaganda and Trotsky's persuasion had done their job well.

You may conclude that the seizure of Petrograd by the Bolsheviks, one of the major turning points in world history, came about through a mixture of skill, incompetence, indifference and luck.

Map showing the stages by which the Bolsheviks seized Petrograd in November 1917.

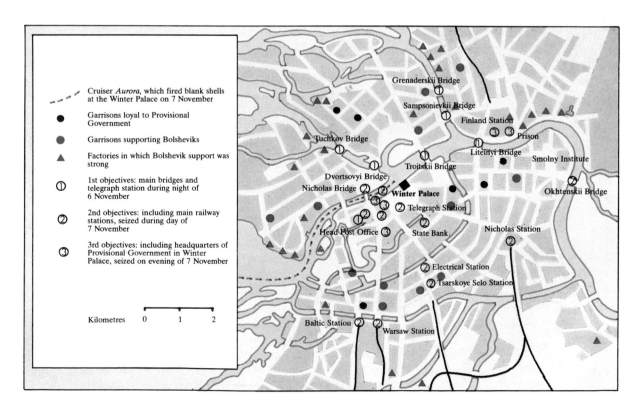

Communist rule

Throughout 1917 the Bolsheviks had criticized the Provisional Government for not calling a Constituent Assembly. Lenin said that its calling was 'one of the three pillars of Bolshevism'. 'Our party alone', he wrote, on taking power, 'can secure the Constituent Assembly's convocation [summoning].'[19] 'Long live the Constituent Assembly!' roared Trotsky in October 1917.[20]

But in December 1917 Lenin wrote:

> ...revolutionary Social Democracy has repeatedly emphasized ...that a republic of Soviets is a higher form of democracy than the usual bourgeois republic with a constituent assembly.

Therefore, he was able, he argued, to dismiss the Constituent Assembly when it met in January because it would not agree with the Soviets, which he had pronounced to be 'a higher form of democracy.'[21] What do you think he meant by this phrase? Lenin certainly seemed to have had the well-being of the Russian people at heart; did this entitle him to dissolve the Assembly elected by the people because he felt that it would not serve their best interests?

If the dismissal of the Constituent Assembly was controversial, the signing of the treaty of Brest-Litovsk was more so. The Russian delegation at the peace talks issued this statement:

> Under the circumstances Russia has no freedom of choice ... The Soviet government ...unable to resist the armed offensive of German imperialism, is forced to accept the peace terms so as to save revolutionary Russia.[22]

So Russia lost 80 per cent of her sugar factories, 73 per cent of her iron and 75 per cent of her coal. In February 1918 a referendum among 200 Soviets had found 105 in favour of war with Germany. By November

Lenin believed that the Russian revolution heralded world-wide communist revolution. This poster shows him ridding the world of all oppressors: monarchs, priests and capitalists.

1918, nine months after Brest-Litovsk, Germany herself had surrendered to the Allies. Had Lenin done the right thing? Was what was best for Russia the same as what was best for the Bolsheviks?

Peace and the calling of a Constituent Assembly had been key points in the Bolshevik programme. In power Lenin took a very different attitude to each.

Throughout 1917 Russia had been slipping further and further into chaos and anarchy. Lenin and the Bolsheviks gradually restored law and order. 'Ideological talk and phrase-mongering about political liberties should be dispensed with' wrote Lenin; 'all that is just mere chatter ...'[23] He believed that building a new world for the people of Russia was more important than the particular needs of any individual. Hence this ferocious order of Cheka, issued in February 1922:

> *Cheka ... 'asks the Soviets to proceed at once to seek out, arrest and shoot immediately all ... (1) agents of enemy spies, (2) counter-revolutionary agitators, (3) speculators, (4) organizers of revolts ... against Soviet government ... — all these are to be shot on the spot ... when caught red-handed in the act.'*[24]

'Only the dictatorship of the proletariat is able to liberate mankind', claimed Lenin.[25] He was organizing that dictatorship.

► Soviet seizure of power was not as easily achieved in some cities as it had been in Petrograd. This photograph shows damage to the Royal Palace in Moscow after the Bolsheviks took it over.

▼ A Bolshevik poster produced in 1919 showing on the left the Tsarist regiments and what they fought for, and on the right the Red Army and what they fight for now. Can you identify what the two different armies are fighting for?

ЦАРСКИЕ ПОЛКИ И КРАСНАЯ АРМИЯ

ЗА ЧТО СРАЖАЛИСЬ ПРЕЖДЕ

ЗА ЧТО СРАЖАЮТСЯ ТЕПЕРЬ

Civil war 1918–21

WITHIN A FEW MONTHS of seizing power, the Bolsheviks (who from March 1917 termed themselves Communists) were faced with widespread and fierce resistance to their regime. There were three elements to this: the Russians who opposed Bolshevism; subject nationalities, such as the Ukrainians, who sought independence from the Russian government; and intervention in the civil war from Allied powers, such as Britain, the USA and Japan. All those who fought against the Bolsheviks are loosely termed the Whites, or counter-revolutionaries. The Communists are known as the Reds.

The White Russians were made up of the many parties who opposed Lenin, such as the Monarchists, Cadets and S.R.s, members of the middle classes, army officers and Cossacks. At first they had consider-

A parade of British troops in Vladivostock in 1918. Although several Allied nations sent troops and equipment to aid the Whites, they were unwilling to let their forces become openly involved in the fighting. What sort of reception are the British receiving from the Russians?

able success. In Moscow and Petrograd the Reds had to contend with a strike of civil servants, and then an attempted S.R. coup in July 1918. When this failed the S.R.s resorted to terrorism, even wounding Lenin himself in August.

While the Reds held fast to the centre of the country, the Whites advanced on the borderlands. In the south, the Ukraine and lands south of the Caucasus declared themselves independent. Here a large White Volunteer Army grew up, led at first by General Alekseev, then by Kornilov and finally by

General Denikin. In the east, around Samara and Kazan, Chernov set up a government, while still further east Admiral Kolchak made considerable advances, adopting the title 'Supreme Ruler of Russia'. 40,000 released Czechoslovakian prisoners of war joined the counter-revolutionary fighting in this area. The Japanese supported break-away movements in Siberia.

To the north the British, French and Americans backed a White government in Archangel. Finally, in the west General Yudenich led a powerful White threat to Petrograd. From Finland, through Estonia, Latvia, Lithuania, Poland and White Russia to the Ukraine, all the small nations on Russia's borders declared themselves independent.

In the end it was Trotsky more than any-one else who saved the Communist state. As War Commissar he headed the Supreme Military Council, a position that he used to introduce conscription and build a Red Army that totalled five million by June 1920. With single-minded ruthlessness he organized the whole country for war. Gradually, one by one, the disunited attackers were defeated.

Denikin fell back in the autumn of 1919 while Trotsky, rushing from front to front in his special command train, drove Yudenich from Petrograd at the same time. Kolchak was captured and shot in February 1920. By May 1921 Poland and the smaller nations to the north had secured independence but Georgia, White Russia and the Ukraine were once more under Communist rule; foreign troops had left Russian soil. The cost had been horrifying, but the revolution had been saved.

The Red Army enters Irkutsk on 7 March 1920, having routed Kolchak's army. This victory by the Red Army brought to an end the White Guard counter-revolutionary regime in Siberia, the Urals and the Far East.

White weaknesses

Careful study of the map below affords a good insight into the weaknesses of the White counter-revolutionary forces during the civil war. Consider, for example, the advance of General Denikin in the Ukraine during the summer of 1918 and in 1919. He was in a position to cut off Moscow's vital grain supplies from the south and he might have brought the war to a victorious close for the Whites if he had managed to link with the Czechs, who at that time were in Samara and Kazan.

There were several factors preventing the Whites from operating in unison. Their armies were widely dispersed and contact

▲ A poster from about 1918–19 entitled 'Capitalists of all countries unite'.

between them was difficult. The technology did not exist for easy co-ordination and the problem was compounded by the fact that so many different languages were spoken within the White forces.

Mention of the Czechs raises the question of foreign help for the Whites. Above is a Soviet cartoon of 1919. Entitled 'Capitalists of all countries unite', it is a clear attack on foreign intervention in the civil war. Which are the three powers represented? According to the artist, who are the victims of the foreign intervention? By implication, the cartoon is trying to put over the message that the Reds are the true patriots and that anyone who supports the Whites is a traitor.

One incident during the civil war highlights another problem faced by the Whites.

◄ Map showing the movements of Red and White armies during the civil war.

In September 1918 there was a conference of anti-Bolshevik parties at Omsk, a town on the Trans-Siberian Railway to the east of the Urals. As a result of this meeting an all-Russian Directory of five members was established to run the government and direct the counter-revolutionary forces in the east of Russia. Prominent on this committee of ex-Constituent Assembly members was Victor Chernov, the S.R. leader. However, the Directory lasted only two months. In November there was a military coup. The new government was suppressed for being too radical, and power in the area passed to Admiral Kolchak. Chernov was saved by the Czechs, but other members of his group were killed.

The interventionists showed little mercy towards those who they suspected of sympathizing with the Bolsheviks. These are bodies of workers employed at a station near Murmansk, who were shot by the British army.

Finally consider this description of what became known as the 'White fury' – the cruelty of the White forces when they recaptured an area from the Reds:

> *... The mounted platoon entered the village, met the Bolshevik committee, and put the members to death ... After the execution the houses of the culprits were burned and the male population under forty-five whipped soundly ... Then the population was ordered to deliver without pay the best cattle, pigs, fowl, forage and bread for the whole detachment, as well as the best horses.*[26]

Remember that the Soviets had given the peasants land, thus making them unwilling to support the counter-revolutionaries. The kind of behaviour by the Whites recorded above cannot have helped their cause.

Red strengths

Tony Cliff, a modern socialist writer, has written in glowing terms of the part played by Trotsky in organizing and inspiring the Red victory in the civil war:

> *Trotsky was the father of the Soviet victory. He was the founder of the Soviet army and the artisan of its victories. He undertook to create a massive and powerful army out of practically nothing. He galvanized the huge numbers of workers and peasants in the Red Army, strengthened their will for victory, stiffened their morale and led them to victory . . . Trotsky's gifts were a rare combination of organization and improvisation, coupled with a genius for making the soldiers know and love what they were fighting and dying for.*[27]

Some readers might consider this passage rather too strong in its praise of Trotsky: consider the author's use of words like 'victory', 'genius' and 'love'. Compare Cliff's passage with this from another expert on Russian history:

> *The first years of the Soviet regime have justly become a legendary Communist epic . . . Yet, a closer look puts the picture into a better focus and helps to explain the Bolshevik victory without recourse to magic in Marxism or superhuman qualities of Red fighters . . . The Reds . . . had advantages that in the end proved decisive. The Soviet government controlled the heart of Russia, including both Moscow and Petrograd, most of its population, much of its industry, and the great bulk of the military supplies intended for the First World War. The White armies constantly found themselves outnumbered and, in spite of Allied help, more poorly equipped. Also, the Red Army enjoyed the inner lines of communication . . . Still more important, the Reds possessed strict unity of command . . .*[28]

An idealistic Bolshevik poster showing the working classes triumphing over capitalism.

An anti-civil war poster produced in 1919. In the top part are Denikin, Yudenich and Kolchak. Below, Denikin and Yudenich are being strangled by the proletariat. What is the poster saying to anyone who may doubt the revolutionary cause?

This passage is less emotive than the first. Some may find it almost cynical; for example, why did the author use the words 'magic' or 'epic'? Which writer offers a more truthful explanation of events? Why?

The majority of Russians were simple peasants. They cared little for Red or White ideology. Indeed, there is evidence of peasants attacking the forces of both sides, wishing to be left in peace. In the last instance, nevertheless, perhaps the Bolshevik prop-aganda put over a message that came closest to the heart of the ordinary Russian peasant. Consider the two posters on this page. The peasants might well have sneered at the idealism of Kocherghin's poster opposite, but the caricature of Generals Denikin and Yudenich, being strangled by the proletariat, would have struck a chord: however difficult the Reds might be, did the peasants really want to return to the old days of gentry landlords and strutting generals?

War communism

The Soviets had immense problems of supply during the civil war. War-time destruction ruined thousands of factories and farms; moreover, the occupation by the Whites of huge areas of Russia and an Allied blockade of her ports meant that many essential raw materials and goods became virtually unobtainable. By 1920, for example, iron production had fallen to about one twelfth of the 1919 level.

The first response of the Soviet government was to print millions of rouble notes. But the more paper money there was about, the more prices rose. Inflation soared, so that by October 1920 each rouble was worth only one hundredth of its November 1917 value. The peasants, therefore, unwilling to sell their produce for worthless notes, cut production to provide a sufficient amount only for themselves and their families.

Faced with this crisis, the government took complete control of the economy. All major industries, from textile production to tobacco processing, were nationalized. On 19 February 1918, all land was deemed to belong to the state, and each village was made responsible for providing the quota of food demanded by the Commissariat of Supplies. Life was very hard for the ordinary Russian under war communism. Food was rationed, strikes were banned, people had to work where they were told and anyone suspected of disagreeing with the system was liable to be dealt with by Cheka.

During the civil war agriculture was severely disrupted and all supply lines were directed towards continuing the war in defence of the revolution. The real victims of the civil war were the countless Russians who starved or who were made homeless as a result of it.

Red sailors stop a car to check documents; at this time no one was above suspicion.

In January 1920 Emma Goldman, an anarchist who had been born in Lithuania, returned to Russia from the USA. She was put in charge of some convicted speculators:

> They were no speculators, they protested: they were starving, they had received no bread in two days. They were compelled to go out into the market to sell matches or thread to secure a little bread.[29]

She returned to the USA two years later convinced that 'the Bolsheviki now proved themselves the most pernicious [wicked] enemies of the Revolution.'[30]

The picture above of Red sailors checking documents during the October Revolution indicates the degree to which the Red Guard controlled life in Russian cities. But Dzerzhinsky, the head of Cheka, was quite open about what he was doing:

> We stand for organized terror – this should be frankly admitted. Terror is an absolute necessity during times of revolution, our aim is to fight against the enemies of the Soviet Government . . .[31]

And Lenin himself later confirmed:

> There was no other way out . . . We must state quite definitely that, in pursuing our policy, we may have made mistakes and gone to extremes in a number of cases. But in the war-time conditions then prevailing, the policy was in the main a correct one. We had no alternative . . .[32]

The New State 1922–24

FROM THE MIDDLE OF 1921 the Soviet government could finally begin to rebuild its shattered country. The new state was smaller than the Tsarist regime had been: large tracts of the former empire had become free independent states, while in the south both Romania and Turkey had absorbed Russian territory. The remaining area was originally entitled the Russian Soviet Federated Socialist Republic (RSFSR), but in December 1922 this was changed to the now familiar USSR (Union of Soviet Socialist Republics).

The Soviet state was governed by a network of Soviets. At the centre was the All Russia Congress of Soviets, its Executive Committee and the Council of People's Commissars. Soviets were elected, but only members of the Communist Party could stand and the votes of industrial workers counted for more than those of other citizens. Since everyone in a position of importance had to be a member of the Communist party, the party's Central Committee and Politburo controlled all political activity. Lenin, Trotsky, Zinoviev, Stalin and other Communist leaders held the key positions in both government and party.

Although the civil war was over Cheka continued its grisly work, seeking out counter-revolutionaries, censoring the press and ensuring that the party line was followed unswervingly. Spying, torture, concentration camps and summary executions were all part of its weaponry. In 1922 its name was changed to the GPU, which became OGPU in 1924.

It is important not to be too negative about the new Soviet state. Following months of demonstrations of discontent, in March 1921 the sailors of the Kronstadt naval base rose in revolt. They demanded an end to strict economic controls, and free elections to the Soviets and a constituent assembly. Although the Red Army smashed the revolt with ruthless efficiency, Lenin sensed the danger and introduced his New

Feliks Dzerzhinsky, the fanatical head of the Soviet secret police between 1917 and 1924. His organization, first known as Cheka, then changed to the GPU and finally OGPU, became world famous for its policy of ruthless terror.

Economic Policy. Gradually, although shortages and starvation remained, the Soviet economy began to recover. Under communism striking inequalities of wealth were removed. Education was given a high priority and some branches of the arts were encouraged.

Before his death from a stroke in 1924, Lenin was also able to see the first tentative links forged between the USSR and the outside world. Although most nations remained hostile or, at best, suspicious of the USSR, both Britain and Germany made treaties with her in 1921. Relations with Britain then deteriorated when a Conservative government took office, but the 1922 Rapallo treaty confirmed the resumption of Russo-German friendship. Gradually, the world's first communist state was coming out of isolation.

One of the last pictures taken of the Tsar and his family while they were prisoners of the Bolsheviks in Siberia. In July 1918 the whole family was shot in a cellar in Ekaterinburg. Later Lenin ordered the execution of those responsible for the murder.

The New Economic Policy

Seven years of war, revolutions and civil strife in Russia inevitably had a disastrous impact on the economy. These figures show this quite clearly: by 1921 Russian industrial output was one fifth of the 1913 level, iron production had fallen to a mere two per cent of its pre-war level. The harvest yield was 37 per cent of normal, 10 million horses and 20 million cattle had perished. By 1920 the US dollar bought 1,200 roubles.

In February 1921 the Soviet regime faced a rebellion by the masses of workers and members of the armed forces who had brought them to power. A strikers' proclamation ran:

> *A complete change is necessary in the policies of the Government. First of all, the workers and peasants need freedom. They don't want to live by the decrees of the Bolsheviks . . . Determinedly and in an organized manner demand: liberation of all arrested Socialists and non-partisan working men; abolition of martial law; freedom of speech, press and assembly . . .*[33]

Lenin did not grant the freedoms demanded, but he organized a complete change in Russia's economic policy:

> *From now on, by the decision of the All-Russian Soviet Central Executive Committee and the Council of People's Commissars, requisitioning is abolished and a tax in kind in agricultural products is introduced in its place. This tax must be smaller than the requisitions. It must be fixed before the spring planting, so that each peasant may reckon in advance what part of the harvest he must give to the state and what part will remain in his full possession.*[34]

To tackle the severe problems in agriculture meant decentralizing state control of the land, giving the peasants a degree of independence and providing incentives to produce more.

The First World War and the civil war wrought havoc with Russian industry. The Bolsheviks promised to restore the economy and to make the USSR a major industrial country. This poster shows some of the sort of enterprises they hoped to create. Can you name any?

Lenin called his new system 'State Capitalism'. He claimed that it was a 'transition period' between capitalism and communism, a retreat so that Russia could then 'run and leap forward more vigorously'.[35] By 1928 Russian industrial production and the amount of land under cultivation had returned to pre-war levels. Do you think that Lenin really believed in a 'transition period', or had he accepted reality and changed the economic policy to save the country? Did the introduction of the New Economic Policy show that Communism had failed?

◀ In 1921 it is estimated that 25 million Russians were starving, five million of them dying between 1921 and 1922. This poster is entitled 'Remember the starving'. Who do you think it is directed at?

◀ Starving children were a common sight in 1922 during the civil war. What will happen to them when the cruel Russian winter strikes?

The New Order

J. P. Nettl wrote of the early history of the Soviet state:

> . . . the same period witnessed an unprecedented effervescence of experiments in a number of fields which were just as important as politics. Education, literature, painting, music, all seemed to burst out of the constraint of a tired, aristocratically inhibited society which had weighed heavily on the creative atmosphere in Russia since the turn of the century.[36]

In particular, people remark on the skill and originality of the Bolshevik propaganda posters, such as that entitled 'Capital' shown below.

For women the new regime offered new freedom. They were given the same status as men before the law; marriage and divorce were easily accomplished. Some of the more radical sections of society expressed their liberation by advocating free love. Alexandra Kollontai, standing in the right of the picture (opposite), had been in exile with Lenin and became a member of the Bolshevik central committee where she established a Women's Department. She then served as a diplomat in several Soviet embassies abroad. All her life she and like-minded Russian women strove to ensure that in employment, education and status women were given a fair deal. As a result women in the USSR were probably given

Bolshevism established a new order in Russia, based on a simple but popular rejection of capitalism. This Bolshevik poster entitled 'Capital' shows the capitalist in his web of profit. What do you imagine would be its appeal to a Russian worker?

► A Bolshevik poster encouraging Soviet citizens to support the drive for educational advance. Which symbols does the poster use? Do you think it has a strong appeal?

▼ Alexandra Kollontai, the Bolshevik campaigner for reform, (right) and Emma Goldman (left).

ЧТОБЫ БОЛЬШЕ ПРОИЗВОДИТЬ- НАДО БОЛЬШЕ ЗНАТЬ

more equal treatment with men than in any other country in the world.

When the British Labour politician, George Lansbury, visited Russia in 1920 he was delighted with what he saw. 'No set of men and women,' he wrote:

> . . . responsible for a revolution of the magnitude of the Russian Revolution ever made fewer mistakes or carried their revolution through with less interference with the rights of individuals, or with less terrorism and destruction, than the men in control in Russia.[37]

Nowhere else in the world was there a law ordering all citizens between the ages of eight and fifty, who could not read or write, to attend state literacy schools. There was compulsion, but all was done for the good of the people.

But can people be forced to be free? Emma Goldman was in Russia at the same time as George Lansbury. When she left in 1921 she wrote:

> My heart was heavy with the tragedy of Russia. One thought stood out in bold relief: I must raise my voice against the crime committed in the name of the Revolution.[38]

The significance of the revolution

Peasants switching on an electric light for the first time in 1928. After the ravages of the civil war Russia made great advances in raising the standard of living of the ordinary people.

Historians will never agree on the significance of the Russian Revolution. For the historian, David Shub, who participated in the 1905 revolution and who knew Lenin personally, the Bolshevik revolution heralded an era of dark repression:

The trade unions became an appendage of the Party machine and the independent workers' co-operatives were completely eliminated. At the same time, Lenin's political police perfected a system of internal espionage that blanketed Russia with a network of agents far more efficient than the Tsarist Okhrana. Iron clad censorship imposed silence on all criticism of Lenin's policies. The press, radio, cinema and theatre became, for the first time in history, an exclusive instrument of state propaganda. And the prison and concentration camps were filled with far more prisoners than under any of the Tsars. Kronstadt had marked the last great revolt of the Russian people. Henceforth, Lenin's dictatorship was secure. The totalitarian state was coming into being.[39]

◄ The Soviets were very keen that all citizens should have the right to learn to read and write. Even the older members of the community, as those shown here, were taught.

► Some Bolsheviks believed that they should consolidate the revolution in the USSR before trying to spread communism to other countries. Others believed that the Russian Revolution was the first stage in a world-wide communist movement. Which group do you think this poster supports?

This was written in 1948 by a man who had fled from the USSR, at a time when the world had just fought a long war to defeat Hitler's totalitarian state. Furthermore, it then looked as if yet another war might break out between Stalin's totalitarian Soviet Union and the West.

Christopher Hill, however, writing at almost the same time as Shub, took a totally different view. He wrote of three major influences of the Russian Revolution:

1 The 'soviet experience in the bringing of modern civilization to backward peoples';

2 'The USSR has demonstrated in practice that socialism is a system which can work even under the most unpromising conditions';

3 'The Russian Revolution has demonstrated that the common people of the earth . . . can take over power and run the state infinitely more effectively than their 'betters'.'

Hill continues:

> I came back continually to this feature of the Russian Revolution, that it uplifted the poor and the downtrodden and improved their lot in the everyday things of life. This is what most impresses in contemporary records of the revolution and this is what is likely to be its most widespread and lasting effect. For the everyday things of life still mean most to the poor and downtrodden, and they are still the majority of the population of the world.[40]

Leading figures

Empress Alexandra (1872–1918) Tsarina of Russia 1894–1918

Alexandra, a granddaughter of Queen Victoria, was born a princess of Hess-Darmstadt in Germany. She married the young Tsar Nicholas II in 1894 and from then on continually exercised a powerful influence over her husband, particularly in reinforcing his conservative views. Alexandra was a passionate and deeply religious woman, devoted to her husband and her family. When an uncouth holy man named Rasputin seemed to be able to help her son's haemophilia through hypnosis, she did not hesitate to make him welcome at court. This, together with her German ancestry, her influence over the Tsar and her cold manner, made her very unpopular in Russia during the First World War. Along with her husband, the heir Alexis and his three sisters, she was shot by the Bolsheviks at Ekaterinburg in 1918.

Brusilov, Aleksey A. (1853–1926) General

This able soldier served with the cavalry in the Balkans, 1877–8, then in the Russo-Japanese War, 1904–5. He commanded the successful advance of the Russian Eighth Army into Austrian Galicia in 1914, but was forced to withdraw before more powerful forces the following spring. In March 1916 he was appointed overall commander of the south-western front, a position he used to launch a successful attack on Austrian positions in June. 250,000 Austrians were captured, the Romanians were persuaded to join the Allies, and pressure was taken off the western front. Brusilov's command continued under the Provisional Government, and he managed to remain in favour with the Reds after the November 1917 revolution. He was appointed military adviser during the 1920 Polish campaign. In his later years he was an inspector of cavalry and he established a stud farm for cavalry horses outside Moscow.

Denikin, Anton I. (1872–1947) General

After joining the army at fifteen, Denikin rapidly rose through the ranks to be a Lieutenant-General by February 1917. He had been a stern critic of the Romanov court and commanded the western sector of the front for the Provisional Government from March–May, before being moved to the Ukraine. He was imprisoned for supporting Kornilov's revolt but escaped to lead a White army in the Caucasus and the Ukraine, receiving considerable British help. In 1919 his forces came within 402 kilometres of Moscow before being forced back by the Bolsheviks. Denikin was an unswerving patriot who refused to work with the anti-Communist Poles and who wasted his power on combatting breakaway Georgian nationalists while he was fighting the Bolsheviks. He finally fled from the Caucasus in 1920 and died in exile in the USA.

Kerensky, Alexander F. (1881–1971) Democratic Socialist Revolutionary

Alexander Kerensky studied law in St Petersburg. In 1912 he was elected to the Duma as a Labour (Socialist) member. Later he joined the Socialist Revolutionary Party and served as Deputy-Chairman of the Petrograd Soviet. In March 1917 he joined the Provisional Government as Minister of Justice, moving to the War Ministry in May, and finally becoming Prime Minister in July. He misjudged the mood of the Russian people, continuing the war with Germany, failing to call a Constituent Assembly, and underestimating the threat from the Marxist revolutionaries. After an unsuccessful attempt to recapture Petrograd from the Bolsheviks in November 1917, he fled abroad to France and eventually settled in the USA.

Kolchak, Alexander V. (1870(?)–1920) Russian Admiral

After distinguished service during the Russo–Japanese War (1904–5), Admiral Alexander Kolchak commanded the Tsar's Black Sea fleet. He strongly opposed the Bolsheviks, overthrowing a socialist government to the east of the Urals in the winter of 1918 and taking command of the area for the Whites, where he was known as 'Supreme Ruler of Russia'. At the end of 1919 Kolchak handed over his power to General Denikin. A few weeks later he was captured by the Bolsheviks and shot in February 1920.

Kornilov, Lavr G. (1870–1918) General

Lavr Kornilov first made a name for himself commanding a Cossack force in the Russo–Japanese War. In 1914 his division penetrated far into Austria–Hungary but the next year he was captured as the Russians fell back. After a daring escape he was raised to the rank of general and put in charge of the Petrograd district in March 1917, in the capacity of which he arrested Nicholas II. For a few months in the summer of 1917 he was commander-in-chief on the south-western front but, partly through a misunderstanding and partly because he was exasperated by Kerensky's failure to act positively against the Bolsheviks, in September he attempted a right-wing coup in Petrograd against both the Provisional Government and the Soviets. The Red Guards played an important part in Kornilov's defeat, and the general was put under arrest by Kerensky. Escaping after the Bolshevik revolution in November, he fought for Denikin's Whites in the south until he was killed in action in July 1918.

Lenin, Vladimir Ilyich (1870–1924) Leader of the Bolshevik Party

While Lenin was still a young man, his elder brother Alexander Ulyanov (the family name) was hanged for his part in a plot to assassinate Tsar Alexander III. This event had considerable influence on Lenin who, after studying law in Kazan and St Petersburg, was arrested for revolutionary activity in 1897 and exiled to Siberia. From 1900 to 1917, except for the winter of 1905–6, he lived abroad. He wrote extensively about a future socialist revolution, developing the ideas of Karl Marx. He became leader of the Bolshevik (majority) faction of the Social Democrats in 1903 and returned briefly to Russia during the 1905 revolution to organize the St Petersburg Soviet. After the revolution in March 1917 the Germans allowed Lenin to return to Russia, crossing Germany from Switzerland in a sealed train. Lenin's vigorous advocacy of revolution in Petrograd led to the 'July days' – a revolt which he considered premature. After three months in Finland, Lenin again returned to Petrograd to continue to plan for a Bolshevik coup from his headquarters at the Smolny Institute. Following the successful revolution in November 1917 he became head of State as Chairman of the Council of People's Commissars. He used this position to enforce numerous social, economic and political reforms on Russia, also insisting that peace be made with Germany (March 1918). After the defeat of the Whites in the civil war he relaxed his strict 'War Communism' and replaced it with a New Economic Policy (1921). Already weakened by an S.R. assassination attempt in 1918, Lenin now suffered a number of strokes which rendered him incapable of sustained work for the last year of his life. His death in January 1924 finally parted him from his devoted wife and fellow revolutionary, Nadezhda Krupskaya.

Miliukov, Pavel N. (1859–1943) historian and politician

After a distinguished early academic career, Pavel Miliukov became well-known as a liberal, for which he lost his university teaching post in 1895. After travelling abroad, he helped organize the liberals during the 1905 revolution and played a major role in forming the Constitutional Democratic Party. He was critical of Nicholas II's handling of the First World War, forming the moderate Progressive Bloc which called for a government that had the support of the Russian people. Miliukov became Foreign Minister in the Provisional Government until he was forced to resign in May 1917. He fled to the south when the Bolsheviks seized power, working with the White forces before leaving for exile in Paris.

Nicholas II (1868–1918) Tsar of Russia 1894–1917

Nicholas, the son of Tsar Alexander III, was brought up by his father and a conservative tutor, Pobedonostsev. Nicholas married the German princess Alexandra of Hesse in 1894, by whom he had four children, three daughters and a haemophilic son, Alexis. The marriage was close and loving, although both parents were deeply concerned about their sick son, the heir to the Russian imperial throne. Nicholas had little time for ideas of reform but he took very seriously his job of personally ruling his empire. He read all important government papers and even tried out army equipment himself. During the revolution of 1905 he gave way to demands for reform only when forced to do so, agreeing to summon a form of parliament called the Duma. Twice during his reign he unwisely allowed his empire to be drawn into war, against Japan in 1904 and against the Central Powers in 1914. In September, 1915 Nicholas personally assumed supreme command of his armies. This focused criticism of military

failure upon himself. He found it difficult to know whom to trust, frequently changing ministers and listening to poor advice, the best example of which was the influence wielded at court between 1905 and 1916 by the monk Rasputin. The last Tsar was forced to abdicate on 15 March 1917. He was then kept under guard at his palace of Tsarskoe Selo until August 1917, before being moved to Siberia and finally to Ekaterinburg in the Urals. It was here that Nicholas and all his family were executed by the Bolsheviks on 16 July 1918.

Rasputin, Grigory (1871–1916) peasant mystic

Grigory Rasputin had no formal education but over the first thirty years of his life he acquired a reputation as a holy man (starets) with powers of healing. From 1905 onwards he exercised some influence at court because it was found that his hypnotic powers could help the sufferings of the haemophilic heir to the throne, Alexis. Despite the scandals of drunkenness and debauchery that surrounded him, Rasputin remained in favour with the Tsar and his wife until he was murdered in 1916 by a group of aristocrats.

Stalin, Joseph V. (1879–1953) Bolshevik revolutionary

Joseph Stalin (born Joseph Djugashvili) came from Georgia, where he was associated with revolutionary politics from an early age. He was exiled to Siberia in 1903 and soon joined the Bolshevik faction of the S.D.s. When the Provisional Government was established in March 1917 he became editor of the Bolshevik newspaper, *Pravda* (Truth), helping with the November revolution and becoming Commissar for Nationalities at the end of the year. During the civil war he played an important part

a time in exile in Siberia, then escaped to become leader of the revolutionary Mensheviks abroad. After the March 1917 revolution Trotsky returned to Russia, became a Bolshevik and played a vital part in organizing the Bolshevik seizure of power in November. As Commissar for Foreign Affairs he negotiated the Treaty of Brest-Litovsk with Germany (March 1918), delaying as long as possible in the hope that Communist revolution would spread to Germany and Austria–Hungary. During the civil war he became Commissar for War and played a key role in organizing the successes of his Red Army. Preoccupied with war and foreign affairs, Trotsky lost touch with internal party matters so that Stalin was able to outmanoeuvre him after Lenin's death. Deported in 1929, Trotsky was eventually killed in Mexico by Stalin's agents. (See picture below).

in the fighting around Petrograd and Tsaritsyn (later re-named Stalingrad). From 1922 onwards he was General Secretary of the Communist Party, a position he used to build up considerable power and support in the party. From this base he was able to seize the leadership of the USSR after Lenin's death. (See picture above).

Trotsky, Lev (1879–1940) Bolshevik revolutionary

After early involvement in revolutionary activity, in 1897 Lev Trotsky (who came from a Ukrainian Jewish family called Bronstein) was arrested. Five years later he joined Lenin in London in 1902, but sided with the Mensheviks when the S.D.s split. In 1905 he was back in St Petersburg helping organize the first Soviet. He was arrested when the revolution was suppressed, spent

Important dates

Note:
Until 1918 Russia used the Julian Calender, which was thirteen days behind the rest of Europe. All the dates here are in the Gregorian Calender in use elsewhere in Europe.

Events

Date	Russia		Rest of World
1861	Emancipation of privately owned serfs.	1854–6	Crimean War: ends in defeat for Russia.
1870	Vladimir Ilyich Ulyanov (Lenin) born.	1870–71	Franco–Prussian War: ends in defeat for France.
1873	Populists try to educate the peasants in revolutionary ideas.		
1881–94	Reign of the conservative Alexander III, father of Nicholas II.		
1894	Nicholas II becomes Tsar. Franco–Russian Treaty.		
1898	Social Democratic Party (S.D.s) formed.		
1901	Trans-Siberian Railway opened.		
1902	Socialist Revolutionary Party (S.R.s) founded.		
1903	S.D.s divided into Bolsheviks and Mensheviks.		
1904–5	Russo–Japanese War: Russia defeated.	1904	Anglo–French Entente Cordiale.
1905	*22 January* 'Bloody Sunday': striking workers fired on by troops; revolution breaks out. *30 October* Nicholas II gives way to revolutionary demands and grants a constitution.		
1906	First Duma met, but dissolved after 73 days. Peter Stolypin, Minister of the Interior and Prime Minister, begins agrarian and other reforms.	1906	Liberal Government comes to power in Britain.
1907	Second Duma met for 102 days Third Duma (to 1912). Lenin in Switzerland.	1908	Anglo–Russian Entente.
1911	Stolypin assassinated by S.R.s.	1911	Revolution in China.
1912–17	Fourth Duma, from whose members the Provisional Government was largely formed. *Pravda* first published.		
1914	Rasputin returns to court from Siberia. Russia declares war on Germany. Russia defeated at battles of Tannenburg and Masurian Lakes.		*August–September* First World War begins.
1915	*August* Nicholas II assumes supreme command of Russian armies. Serbia conquered by Austria and Bulgaria.		*December* Gallipoli attack fails.
1916	*June* Brusilov's successful offensive against Austria. *December* Rasputin assassinated.		*January* German assault on Verdun. *July* British offensive on the Somme.
1917	*8 March* Strikes and demonstrations begin in Petrograd. *12 March* Petrograd Soviet formed. *14 March* Soviet issues Order No. 1.		*March* USA declares war on Germany.

Date	Russia	Rest of World
	First Provisional Government formed. Nicholas II abdicates. *April* Lenin arrives in Petrograd. *May* Provisional Government reorganized to include Mensheviks and S.R.s. *June* First All-Russian Congress of Soviets. *July* Kerensky's offensive begins. Cadets leave Provisional Government. *16–18 July* 'July Days': Bolshevik rising (against Lenin's wishes) fails. Lenin leaves Russia. *August* Provisional Government re-formed. *6–10 September* General Kornilov's attempt to seize Petrograd fails. Bolsheviks play a major part in his defeat. *October* Provisional Government re-formed for last time. *6–7 November* Red Guards seize Petrograd. Bolshevik revolution. *7 November* Members of Provisional Government arrested. *December* Armistice with Central Powers. Cheka founded.	*June* Third Battle of Ypres on Western Front.
1918	*January* Constituent Assembly meets; closed the next day. *March* Treaty of Brest–Litovsk signed. Trotsky appointed War Commissar. *May* Communists driven out of Don region. Czechs seize Trans-Siberian Railway. Nicholas II and family shot. *August* Lenin seriously wounded in an S.R. assassination attempt. *November* Kolchak seizes power in Siberia.	*March* Germans begin Ludendorff offensive on Western Front. *November* Ceasefire on the Western Front.
1919	*April* Kolchak's advance on the Volga halted. *June* Denikin begins White seizure of the Ukraine. *October* Denikin 320 km from Moscow. Yudenich's attack on Petrograd fails. *December* Ukraine re-captured by Reds.	*January* Rising of German Communists (Spartacists) fails. *March–August* Communist regime governs in Hungary. *June* Treaty of Versailles signed.
1920	*February* Kolchak executed. Allied troops leave Archangel. *November* Whites driven out of Crimea.	*February* League of Nations first meets.
1921	*February* Georgia reconquered by Bolsheviks. *March* Rebellion by the sailors of the Kronstadt naval base. Lenin launches his New Economic Policy.	
1922	*May* Lenin has his first stroke. *December* Russia becomes the USSR.	*May* Mussolini seizes power in Italy.
1924	*21 January* Death of Lenin.	*January* Labour government comes to power in Britain.

Glossary

Abdicate	To give up the throne, or another responsibility.
Anarchist	One opposed to all formal government.
Authoritarian	A form of governing in which a small élite or one person has dictatorial powers.
Autocracy	Government by a single ruler with unlimited authority.
Bolshevik	The majority party that was formed when the Social Democratic Party split in 1903.
Bourgeoisie	The middle classes.
Bureaucracy	A system of government organized into strict layers of departments and officials.
Cabinet	The most important ministers of a government who decide on policy.
Cadet	A member of the Constitutional Democratic Party, pledged to moderate democratic reforms.
Capitalism	An economic theory that believes in the virtue of free enterprise, and the right to individual property and wealth.
Central Powers	Germany and her allies (Austria–Hungary, Turkey, Bulgaria) in the First World War.
Cheka	The Bolshevik government's secret police.
Coalition	A government that consists of members of more than one party.
Commissar	A communist officer or minister.
Conservative	Someone opposed to excessive or rapid change.
Constitution	The rules by which government is conducted.
Constituent assembly	A representative assembly elected by universal suffrage to represent the people.
Cossacks	A people of south and south-west Russia, famous for their independent spirit and military prowess.
Counter-revolutionary	The phrase used by the communists to describe anyone who opposed them.
Coup	A sudden seizing of power by force.
Currency	Money.
Delegation	A group sent by a large number of people to represent their wishes.
Democracy	Rule by the people or their elected representatives.
Deputy	Someone appointed to act on behalf of others and to put forward their point of view.
Duma	The Russian Parliament 1905–17.
Dynasty	A ruling family.
Emancipation	Setting free.
Georgia	A Russian province in the south-west near Turkey, Iran and the Black Sea.
GPU	State Political Administration – the Soviet police and secret police from 1922–3.
Haemophilia	A disease in which the blood fails to clot.
Imperialism	Aggressive action by a state to take over others.
Inflation	When money loses its value and prices rise faster than incomes.
Liberalism	A philosophy that sets great store by the freedom of the individual and the rule of law.

Martial law	Rule by the military.
Marxism	The ideas of Karl Marx (1818–83) a German philosopher. He claimed to have discovered the laws that govern the behaviour of human society in history: societies move from feudalism, through capitalism to socialism, directed by economic forces. He held that most nineteenth-century states were in a capitalist phase and that revolution was needed to herald in the socialist (communist) era. For its believers, Marxism explains the present and offers hope for the future.
Menshevik	The minority party that was formed when the Social Democratic Party split in 1903. Until 1918 there were more Mensheviks than Bolsheviks in Russia.
Ministry	A government department.
Mobilize	Make ready for war action.
Monarchist	One who supports the idea of government with a king or queen.
Nationalize	The taking over by the state of an industry or service.
Nihilist	An anarchist.
Okhrana	Tsarist secret police.
Politburo	The most important policy-making committee of the Communist Party.
Proletariat	The industrial working classes.
Propaganda	Information slanted to favour one point of view over all others.
OGPU	The Soviet police and secret police from 1923–34.
Provisional Government	The Russian Government of March – November 1917.
Rationing	Limiting food and other commodities in times of hardship.
Referendum	A popular poll, in which the people get a chance to vote for or against a proposal.
Repression	Holding down by force.
Representative assembly	(*see* constituent assembly).
Requisition	To seize on behalf of the state or an army.
Republic	A form of government in which power is held by the people or their elected representatives.
Revenue	The government's income.
Revolution	A complete and permanent change.
Russification	A policy of making all areas of Russia adopt the same culture.
Serf	Unfree peasants who owned no land and who could be bought and sold.
Serfdom	The condition when all peasants are serfs.
Socialism	An economic theory that believes that the state should own all important means of the production and distribution of wealth.
Soviet	An elected council or assembly.
Speculator	Someone who hoards a commodity in the hope that it will be more valuable later.
Tsar	The hereditary emperor of Russia; a form of the word 'Caesar'.
Ukraine	A large Russian province to the north of the Black Sea.
White Russians	Another name for the Belorussians, a people living near the Russo-Polish border.
Whites	The anti-communists.
Winter Palace	The Tsar's palace in St Petersburg (later Petrograd).

Further reading

Text Books
Chamberlin, W. H., *The Russian Revolution 1917–1921* (2 vols), Macmillan, 1935.
Kochan, L., *The Making of Modern Russia,* Penguin, 1970.
Riasanovsky, N. V., *History of Russia,* Oxford, 1977.
Seton-Watson, H., *The Russian Empire, 1801–1917,* Oxford, 1967.

Easier Books
Campling, Elizabeth, *The Russian Revolution,* Batsford, 1985.
Cash, A., *The Russian Revolution,* Benn, 1967.
Footman, D., *The Russian Revolution,* Faber, 1962.
Gibson, Michael, *The Russian Revolution,* Wayland, 1986.
Halliday, H. E., *Russia in Revolution,* Longman, 1972.
Kochan, L., *Lenin,* Wayland, 1974.
Mack, D. W., *Lenin and the Russian Revolution,* Longman, 1970.
Newman, Fred, *Leader of the Russian Revolution,* Wayland, 1981.
Salisbury, Harrison E., *Russia in Revolution,* Deutsch, 1978.
Smith, W. H. C., *The Last Czar,* Wayland, 1973.

Scholarly Works
Carr, E. H., *The Bolshevik Revolution 1917–1923,* (3 vols), Penguin, 1966.
Deutscher, I., *Trotsky,* 3 vols., Oxford 1954–70.
Hill, C., *Lenin and the Russian Revolution,* Pelican, 1971.
Katkov, G., *Russia 1917,* Longman, 1967.
Nettl, J. P., *The Soviet Achievement,* Thames & Hudson, 1967.
Schapiro, L., *1917,* Pelican, 1985.
Shub, D., *Lenin,* Pelican. 1966.
Williams, Beryl *The Russian Revolution 1917–21* Blackwell, Historical Association Studies, 1987.

Original Sources
Bunyan, J. and Fisher, H. H., *The Bolshevik Revolution 1917–1918,* Stanford, 1934.
Kerensky, A. F., *The Kerensky Memoirs,* Cassell, 1966.
Krupskaya, N., *Memoirs of Lenin,* Panther, 1970.
Lenin, V. I., *The Essentials of Lenin,* Lawrence and Lishart, 1947.
McCauley, M., (ed.), *The Russian Revolution and the Soviet State, 1917–1921,* Weidenfeld and Nicholson, 1976.
Reed, John, *Ten Days That Shook the World,* Penguin, 1977.
Trotsky, L., *History of the Russian Revolution,* Gollancz, 1970.
Vernadsky, G. et. al., *A Source Book of Russian History* (3 vols), Yale, 1972.
Wood, A., *The Russian Revolution,* Longman, 1986.

Notes on sources

1 Vorres, Ian , *Last Grand Duchess: The Memoirs of Grand Duchess Olga Alexandrovna*, London, 1964.
2 Florovsky, George cited in Riasanovsky, Nicholas V., *A History of Russia*, (3rd edit.), Oxford, 1977.
3 Cited in Nettl, J. P., *The Soviet Achievement*, London, 1967.
4 Pares, B. (ed.), *Letters of the Tsaritsa to the Tsar*, 1914–1916, London, 1931.
5 *Ibid.*
6 Alexander, Grand Duke of Russia, *Once a Grand Duke*, New York, 1932.
7 Seton-Watson, Hugh, *The Russian Empire 1801–1917*, Oxford, 1967.
8 Pares, *op. cit.*
9 Kerensky, Alexander, *Memoirs*, London, 1966.
10 Schapiro, Leonard, *1917 The Russian Revolutions*, London 1984.
11 Kerensky, *op. cit.*
12 Schapiro, *op. cit.*
13 Kerensky, *op. cit.*
14 Reed, John, *Ten Days that Shook the World*, London, 1961.
15 *Ibid.*
16 *Ibid.*
17 *Ibid.*
18 Schapiro, *op. cit.*
19 Lenin, V. I., *Collected Works*, cited in Cliff, T., *Lenin*, London, 1987.
20 Browder, R. P. and Kerensky, A. F., *The Russian Provisional Government 1917 – Documents*, Stanford, 1961.
21 Lenin, *op. cit.*
22 Bunyan, J. and Fisher, H. H., *The Bolshevik Revolution 1917–1918*, Stanford, 1934.
23 Lenin, *op. cit*, cited in Shub, D., *Lenin*, London, 1966.
24 Bunyan and Fisher, *op. cit.*
25 Lenin, *op. cit.*
26 Drozdovsky, M. G., *Diary of Colonel Drozdovsky*, 1923, cited in Simkin, J., *The Bolshevik Government*, Brighton, 1986.
27 Cliff, T., *Lenin*, London, 1987.
28 Riasanovsky, *op. cit.*
29 Goldman, E., *My Disillusionment in Russia*, New York, 1923.
30 *Ibid.*
31 Cited in Simkin, *op. cit.*
32 Lenin, *op. cit.*
33 Cited in Shub, *op. cit.*
34 From *Pravda*, cited in Simkin, *op. cit.*
35 Lenin, *op. cit.*
36 Nettl, *op. cit.*
37 Lansbury, George, *What I Saw in Russia*, London, 1920.
38 Goldman, *op. cit.*
39 Shub, *op. cit.*
40 Hill, C., *Lenin and the Russian Revolution*, London, 1947.

Picture acknowledgements

The author and publishers would like to thank the following for allowing their illustrations to be reproduced in this book: BBC Hulton Picture Library 6, 9, 19 (bottom), 20 (bottom), 25, 45, 47 (bottom); Beinecke Rare Book and Manuscript Library 16; The Bettmann Archive 35 (top), 49 (left); The Bodleian Library 8; Mary Evans Picture Library 17 (bottom), 55 (bottom); John Freeman & Co. 15, 46; David King Collection cover, 7 (top), 13, 17 (top), 23, 24, 34, 35 (bottom), 38 (top), 41, 43, 51; Mansell 10, 31 (bottom); New York Public Library 48; Novosti 7 (bottom), 11, 12, 14, 20 (top), 21, 26, 27 (top), 28, 30, 31 (top), 36, 37, 39, 42, 44, 50 (top and bottom); Popperfoto 27 (bottom); John Massey Stewart 29, 32, 47 (top), 49 (right); Victoria and Albert Museum 5; Wayland Picture Library 19 (top), 22, 40, 55 (top). The maps were supplied by Malcolm Walker.

Index